Shapes at the Beach

Laura Young

Rosen REAL READERS

Rosen Classroom Books & Materials
New York

1

Can you find the shapes at the beach?

circle

The ball is a small circle.

circle

The umbrella is a big circle.

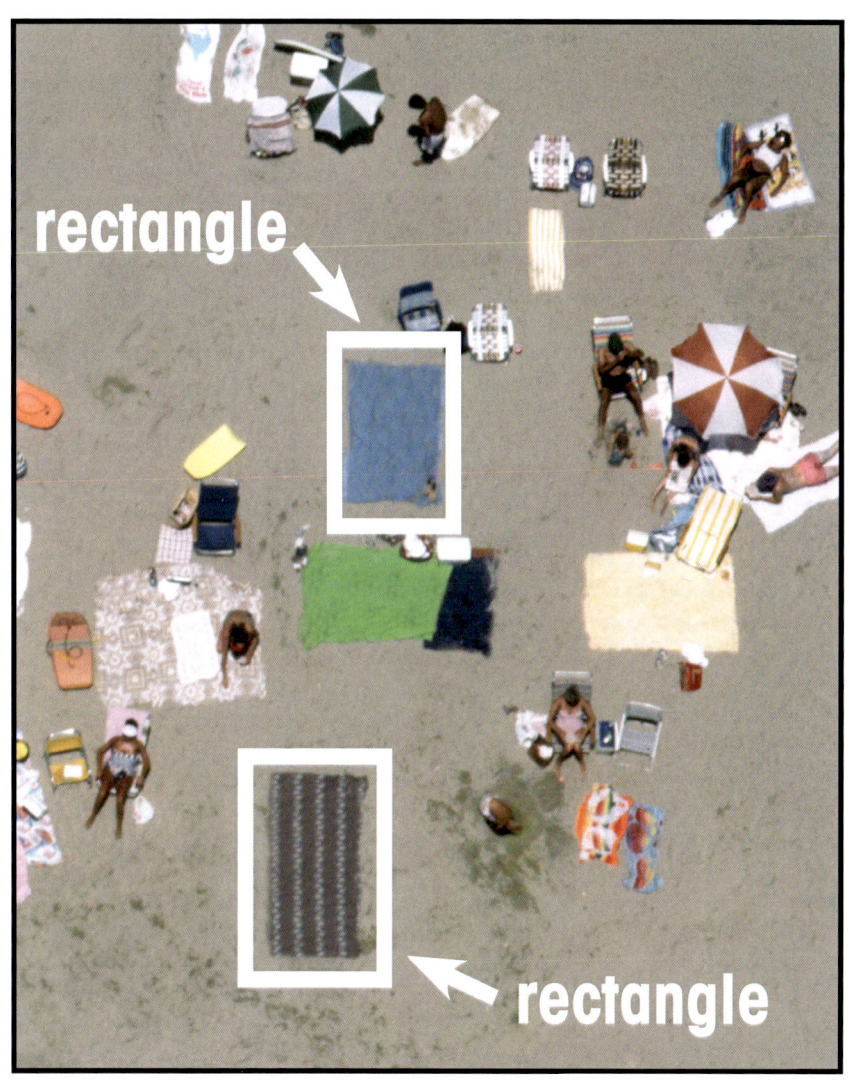

The towels are rectangles.

triangle

The sail is a big triangle.

triangle

The cone is a small triangle.

Words to Know

circle

rectangle

sail

towel

triangle

umbrella